Food For Thought

A Collection of Original Thought-Provoking Poems

DAVE RICHMOND

To order additional copies of this book, contact:
Xlibris
1-888-795-4274
www.Xlibris.com
Orders@Xlibris.com

ISBN: Softcover 978-1-9845-8426-7
EBook 978-1-9845-8425-0

Print information available on the last page

Rev. date: 06/22/2020

Food For Thought

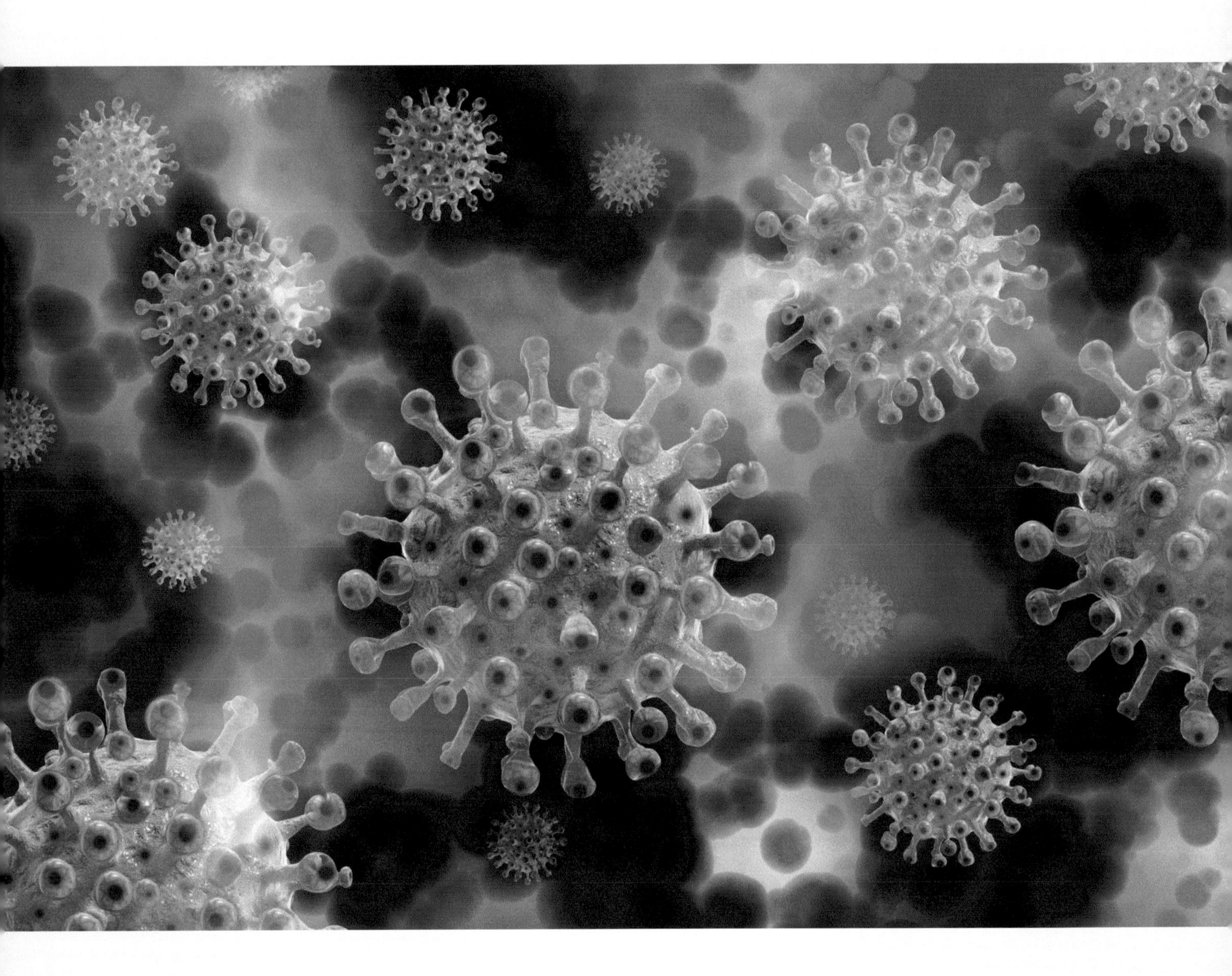

Author's note: This poem was inspired by the Coronavirus pandemic of 2020 and written to help readers think about some of the existential issues that Covid-19 has caused to surface.

1. The Tale of Covid-19

Experts tell us you originated in Wuhan province,
But these days the masses are difficult to convince,
At a time when fake news and conspiracy theories abound,
Tell me where, O where can the truth about you be found.

Your name sounds like something out of a sci-fi horror picture,
And for the past few months you have been a daily news feature,
Dominating the headlines with your insidious spread,
And a daily tabulation of the newly infected and dead.

With lightning-speed you moved from nation to nation,
Filling the hearts of humans with fear and trepidation,
You afflict and kill both young and old
Leaving a trail of grief and economic loss untold.

As a nation we have boasted of our great wealth,
But you have revealed the fragility of our health,
Our formidable weapons and military might,
Are no match for you who are hidden from sight.

You have our experts all scratching their heads,
And our nations hospitals running out of beds.
The way you infect, and kill is so uncanny,
That the number of dead victims will be very many.

You have a nickname, they call you "the Rona"
Some people are scared to call you Corona,
They do not care if they die drinking Coors or vodka,
But no one wants to die because they tasted Corona.

I am amazed that a creature so tiny and small,
Can humble proud nations full of gumption and gall
You have taught us lessons that I hope we will cherish,
As a tribute to our loved ones who by you will perish.

Some good things are happening and here are a few,
Our politicians have united, O, that is so new,
And you have forced us to work together,
So that we can help one another.

The daily news of death has brought us to reality,
And forced us to consider our own mortality,
Social isolation, should not fill us with consternation,
But help us to consider, the reason for our creation.

It is high time for mankind to repent and turn to his maker,
And acknowledge that sin has made death our undertaker,
But our merciful Creator has a plan for our redemption,
Which required the death of Jesus to purchase our salvation.

O God, Creator of earth and firmament,
Look with pity on us the inhabitants of your terrestrial tenement,
We have created corrupt and oppressive forms of government,
And are guilty of destroying the natural environment.

God look down on us your sinful children,
Who have been so unjust to our fellowmen,
Have mercy on us and stop this viral surge
Remove this plague and end the scourge.

Author's Note: This poem was written as a reflection on the shutdown of the American economy and how it has affected our lives. I have a deep suspicion that this may be a dress rehearsal for coming events as expressed in the final stanza.

2. The World in Pause

Incessant motion and constant innovation,
Are the defining features of our modern generation,
The hustle and bustle that drives our economy,
Also help us avoid the ghost of monotony.

But even the great God of all the nations,
After six days of His many creations,
Took time to rest on the seventh day,
As a pattern for those who follow his way.

Six days you should labor is His command,
And rest on the seventh is His demand,
When this day of worship and rest we observe,
We give Father, Son, and Spirit the honor they deserve.

You may say that in today's economy this is not feasible,
But look at what the pandemic has shown to be possible,
The world's economies have almost ground to a halt,
Even though it is not due to their own fault.

Only businesses deemed to be a necessity,
Remain open during this global calamity,
Millions of people who were working before,
Are not gainfully employed anymore.

Businesses once thriving, their doors had to shutter,
Streets that were once buzzing with activity and human chatter,
Are now strangely silent and almost deserted,
And our busses and trains are no longer crowded.

Events long planned have been cancelled or postponed,
Our sports heroes cannot display the skills they have honed,
People once free to move when they wish,
Have been ordered to stay in and not be selfish.

And what is the reason, Oh, what is the cause,
Of this rare phenomenon of a world in pause?
It was ordered by our leaders and enacted by laws,
Designed to check Covid-19 and shut his devouring jaws.

So, when this nightmare is over, and things to normal return,
I hope we will trust God, and his law no more spurn,
By laboring six days and working because,
He said work six days and on the seventh take a pause.

Soon world leaders will enforce Sunday laws in disasters' wake,
To convince us to rest for the environment's sake,
God's law will not change till the heavens the SON shall burst,
He said rest on the seventh and not on the first.

Author's note: This poem was written as a reflection on the shutdown of the American economy and the implications this may have for the future. I believe this may be a dress rehearsal for coming events as powerful forces in the world are working to bring about a new world order.

3. Musings About Life After the Coronavirus Pandemic

I have been thinking about what life in this world might be like,
When from the throes of this pandemic we emerge and take a hike,
Even though we are still in the throes of this global disaster,
One day soon this Coronavirus nightmare we will get over.

Then what will life be like, when Corona vanishes from the landscape,
Would there be unpleasant realities from which we cannot escape?
Will the world economy rapidly recover as many are predicting?
Or could we be in for a prolonged period of economic declining?

Could Covid-19 be the harbinger of future disasters and pandemics,
That will wreak havoc on global economics,
Leading to a period of severe economic distress,
Which makes all our national currencies worthless.

For years some have been predicting a time of universal harmony,
When the whole world would be using one currency,
With the economies of all nations so tightly stretched,
The reality of one world economic order is not far-fetched.

And who would be the leader of this global entity?
It would have to be someone with great moral authority.
Would he or she be Chinese, German, Russian or American?
Or maybe he or she might just be European.

What type of political system might we have to live under?
At this time that might not be too far yonder.
Would we be free to exercise our autonomy?
Or will we become the subjects of an autocracy?

Enough of my musings, but I hope this poem get you thinking,
And start to do some self-evaluating.
The Covid-19 pandemic has made us confront our own mortality,
My sincere hope is that it will also propel us to plan for eternity.

Author's note: This poem was written to honor the sacrifice of healthcare workers, many of whom died during the Coronavirus pandemic.

4. Hail to the Unsung Heroes

We now recognize our healthcare workers as heroes.
Just like soldiers who risk all to conquer their foes.
The Coronavirus pandemic caused the masses to realize,
That in working to save lives, many of these workers have suffered demise,

Like warriors they leave home to enter the fray,
Their calling to save lives they do not betray,
Despite the great obstacles they give of their best,
And work for long hours with no thought of rest.

The battle with Covid-19 has taken a toll,
And many of these heroes have been added to its roll.
Because of their sacrifice many lives have been saved,
Who without their efforts, in a grave would have been laid.

Lord I thank you for these unsung heroes,
Who care for us in our mental and physical woes,
With compassion and skill and the heart of a servant,
Deserving of the honor reserved for the gallant.

Author's note: As I reflected on the Coronavirus pandemic, I thought of the similarities between sin which has been compared to a virus and the Coronavirus. This poem is the product of my reflections.

5. The Coronavirus and the Virus of Sin

When Adam and Eve the forbidden fruit did eat, the world was infected with the virus of sin,
The virus affected the mind of its hosts causing shame, fear, and accusation to seep in,
Adam blamed Eve and she in turn blamed the serpent,
Like them, we, when confronted by sin find it hard to repent.

Like the Coronavirus that is now a pandemic, the virus of sin to this world is endemic,
And the pain, misery, and destruction it causes is sometimes catastrophic,
Killing large numbers of victims in a single occurrence,
And far surpassing the Coronavirus in terms of its prevalence.

Just as the physical effects of a Coronavirus infection can be very serious,
The infection of the sin virus has to the human race been deleterious,
Sickness, death, wars, and famines that result in mass starvation,
Are some of the manifestations of the sin virus infection.

There is no cure for Covid-19 and for many of our maladies,
But the Lord almighty who is the source of all remedies,
Has a solution for the sin virus already designed.
He sent his Son Jesus, who was to death resigned.

So, while the Coronavirus is causing many to despair,
There is no reason the virus of sin to fear,
Just receive the vaccine of the blood of God's Son,
And you will be saved when life here on earth is done.

When the pandemic is over, we do not know what the new normal will be like,
But when the virus of sin is defeated, we know that death will take a hike,
So whatever life is like when things return to what we call normal,
Those who accept the Savior, Jesus, can look forward to life eternal.

Author's note: The inspiration for this poem came to me while vacationing in Cape Cod, Massachusetts. I was captivated by the beautiful sunrises that I experienced each morning from the balcony of my beachfront room. It was originally part of my first poem, Sunrise and Sunset, but then I decided to separate the content into two poems.

6. Sunrise

Like an actor waiting for the curtains to part before the scene unfolds,
She waits below the dark horizon for her appointed time to appear.

The shades of pinkish gray, and bronze and a myriad of color combinations on the horizon, betray her attempt to hide from view.

It is as if she is playing peekaboo with the darkness, tantalizing her audience, mesmerizing them with a symphony of colors.

Suddenly she emerges from beneath the horizon, a sliver of a golden orb, revealing a fraction of herself at a time, all the while painting a scene of indescribable beauty on the canvas of the sky above the line where heaven meets earth.

Once she begins this phase of the drama, there is no hesitation. She is like a giant awakened from slumber and ready to run a race.

Soon this blazing orb of burning gases we call the sun, dispels the darkness of predawn and the earth is aglow with her golden beams.

It is God's plan, that you too should rise and shine like the sun, dispelling darkness wherever it's found.

So, open your heart and let the Son in, then you like the sun will become His channel of light, to those all around you for whom day is still night.

Photos by author

Author's note: The inspiration for this poem came to me while vacationing in Cape Cod, Massachusetts. I was captivated by the beautiful sunsets that I experienced each evening at different places on the Cape. It was originally part of my first poem, Sunrise and Sunset, but then I decided to separate the content into two poems.

7. Sunset

Like a meteor in slow motion, she begins her descent to the abyss below the horizon from which she emerged at sunrise.

As she descends her strength slowly decreases, but her glory does not abate.
About an hour before she vanishes from view, she again plays her tantalizing game.
Descending slowly, like an aircraft touching down on a runway.

She gives the impression that she does not want to exit the stage.
As she nears the horizon, she splashes a dazzling display of colors on the canvass of the sky. The palette of colors and variety of patterns and scenes created by the light and the clouds is as mesmerizing as they were at sunrise.

Finally, this golden ball of fire touches down on the runway of the horizon, resplendent in her glory, turning the horizon to a brilliant orange, burnished bronze and a variety of shades of red and gold all mixed together.

As she sinks below the horizon, she seems to be playing a game of hide and seek as the dark clouds of evening creep over her.

Then suddenly, she is gone, but not without a trace, for her afterglow remains for quite a while after sunset.

Eventually the darkness of night prevails, and we are left with only the memories of another beautiful sunset.

Your life and mine are mirrored by the sun, summarized as it is, as SUNRISE and SUNSET.

It is our Creator's plan that just like the sun, we should leave beautiful memories for loved ones, when our days are done.

So, trust in the Lord with all of your heart and allow Him to direct your path.
Then when at last, your journey ends, you like the sun will leave the afterglow of a life of service to God and your fellowmen.

Photos by author

Author's note: As you can see, this poem radically deviates from the ones you have read so far. I am a deep thinker and spend time contemplating the big questions of life. This poem not surprisingly, came to me as a flash of inspiration while I was engaged in quiet meditation. I am no philosopher, but I am sure that as you read it you will find much food for thought.

8. Silence

Silence is defined as the complete absence of sound, but this definition fails to capture the profundity of the subject.
As humans, our earliest existence is shrouded in obscurity and silence.
Sperm penetrates ovum and zygote forms, initiating a procreative process designed by the Creator - God.
In the liquid-filled tomb of the womb, we take form, like when God created dry land from formless water.

Though surrounded by the constant noise of bodily organs at work, we develop and learn in silence,
As we experience mother's emotions of love or hate, feelings of rejection or acceptance, of joy or sorrow.
We hear her sing and talk and laugh, the good, the bad, we hear it all in the silence of the womb.
Then we are born, and life outside the womb begins. We eat, we grow, we learn and live.

But with each day of life, a miracle is repeated, as busy days give way to restful nights.
As the levels of serotonin and melatonin in our body decrease and increase respectively, we drift into a state of unconscious sleep, and enter the realm of silence once again.

Silence that is essential for our continued existence. For it is during the silence of deep sleep that worn out cells are replaced, depleted energy restored, and the life force replenished.

Then there are times when we retreat for periods of meditation to a secluded place.
In this metaphysical realm of silence, thoughts, ideas, dreams and memories filed away in our subconscious mind, percolate into the conscious mind.

It is during such moments that we connect with our Creator, the source of life, the One who gives life meaning and purpose, the reason for our being, the essence of our existence.
As the silence of sleep is essential to our mental and physical wellbeing, so is the silence of meditation to our emotional, mental and spiritual health.

And what of those times when for reasons unknown to science, our bodies retreat into a comatose state of silence.
When with eyes wide open we do not see, or with eyes shut tight we behold scenes of celestial beauty.
And though unconscious, we can hear what is spoken though we cannot respond with words but only with a gentle squeeze of hand.

Then there is the ultimate silence. The silence of death, the culmination of our life on this earth.
Life is bookended by silence in gestation and silence in death. The key to a meaningful life is to discover the purpose of the period between the bookends.
Without a Supreme Creator in the picture, the period between the bookends lacks meaning and purpose.

Those who find true meaning and fulfillment and purpose in life, are the ones who spend time in the silence of meditation each day, getting to know their Creator and learning about His purpose and plan for their lives.

I challenge you to explore the major philosophies and worldviews, and rigorously interrogate their premises. Analyze their answers to the questions of origin, purpose, meaning, morality and destiny.
Test these answers to see how they play out in the real world. Do they pass the test of coherence? Do they make sense?

My search has led me to the conclusion that the answers provided by the Judeo-Christian worldview make the most sense, therefore, I spend time each day in silence, meditating on the wisdom found in the Bible and communicating with God my Creator, in prayer.

Silence! Silence!! Silence!!! It is indeed golden to the wise who discover and utilize its life-transforming benefits.

Author's note: This poem is a variation on the theme of my poem on silence and is written as an ode. It is my hope that this poem will cause you to think deeply about the origin and purpose of your life and its ultimate destiny.

9. Ode to Silence

O primordial prelude, thou ancient sound, present before the earth was formed. Interrupted by the voice of One who predated you, saying, "let there be," and then allowing you to witness His creative power at work.

O ubiquitous companion, witness of the moment when sperm penetrated ovum and zygote was formed. You saw me before I entered my mother's consciousness and beheld the formation of my members.

Thou welcome interlude, who daily rescue me from the exhaustion of the incessant demands of daily life. As a soothing massage to an aching body, you cradle me in your arms and restore my body and soul.

O divine command used by God to get the attention of His children. "Be still and know that I am God" (Psalm 46:10), He says, and we tremble and are silent in His presence.

O inevitable postlude, the destiny of mortal man. "His spirit departs, he returns to the earth, in that very day his thoughts perish" Psalm 146:4 and he enters your world of silence.

But because you were there when God made man, you were privy to the plan that man should live eternally. So, you are content to hold him fast, till he is resurrected by His Savior at last.

Author's note: This was my first attempt at writing poetry even though I did not know it when I wrote these words as part of a competition to select a song for my high school. At the time when I wrote it in 1986, I had graduated from this school, gone on to college and had returned as an Agricultural Science teacher. My submission was selected as the school song and I also composed the music for the song. As far as I know, it is still sung daily by the students at this school in the land of my birth, Guyana.

It Is included in this book because the school of which I wrote still occupy a special place in my memory.

10. A Hymn for my School

A place where peace and love prevail.
Though patience often fail
Where unity is manifest, and hatred laid to rest.

Refrain:
This is my school, a treasured place.
For boys and girls of every race.
I love my school, 'twill always be,
A treasured place for me.

This school the minds of students train,
Deep things to contemplate.
The hands to labor and to toil, with skill appropriate.

God, bless the students of this school,
The head and teachers too.
Give them the wisdom from above, love for the job they do.

Author's note: This poem is my attempt to present an apologetic for why I believe in God. I hope the readers of this poem will take the time to explore the many valid reasons that have been advanced by intelligent men and women for believing in God.

11. Invisible Realities

Modern living and its obsession with materialism has conditioned us to think that what we can see, and feel is all that is real.

We say, 'seeing is believing' and insist on proof by saying, 'show me' as if to say, 'If we cannot see it and touch it, then for us, it is 'no deal.'

Well, let us test this hypothesis to see if it is true, because the outcome my friends may be important to you.

Can you see the air? Are you sure it is there? You cannot see it, you say, so maybe we have believed a lie.
But if there is no air, then neither you nor I can survive, because without air we all would surely die.

And what about gravity, can you prove it exists? Then show me the proof so that I can believe.
If I jump from a roof would I soar or fall? The answer is not difficult for the mind to conceive.
So now that we agree, that the real may not be seen, let us consider some realities that are unseen.

There is electricity, ultraviolet light, high frequency sound, radiation, vitamins, ova, sperms,
feelings of hurt, pain, rejection, love, hate. bacteria, viruses, and many other types of germs.
Then there is God, heaven, angels, spiritual conversion, demons, visions, miracles .....

When I mention God many ask me, have you ever seen him? And when I say "no", then comes the familiar retort, "Since you, me nor anyone else has never seen him, then I do not believe he is real."

So again, I am forced to ask, does the fact that we cannot see God prove he does not exist?
Have you seen everything you believe? These are questions we cannot resist.

Remember, we agreed that air and gravity are real even though you, I, nor anyone else has ever seen either.

Now this is what I want to say to you; let us be reasonable and intellectually honest and admit, that the age-old, worn-out and popular argument for not believing God is real, is weak and illogical.

If you choose not to believe in God, that is fine! But do not criticize and condemn those who believe. There are many valid reasons to believe in God and they are all considered to be rational.

First empirical, next consciousness, then Aquinas five ways, the dialectical, the inductive and ontological.
So, I hope we can all agree that things do not have to be seen to be real. In fact, if you take the time to consider, you may discover that there are more invisible realities than realities that are visible.

Author's note: I was inspired to write this poem as I was driving through Massachusetts on my way to a vacation in Rhode Island. As I drove along that night, it dawned on me that there was a full moon that seemed to be following my wife and I as we drove along. We were both fascinated by the beauty of the full moon and I told my wife that when we reached our destination, I would write a poem on the moon. Ode to the moon, is the product of my reflections from that experience.

12. Ode to the Moon

Oh, thou "Lesser Light," created by the Master's voice on the fourth day of creation to provide light at night.
Your greater companion, the sun, marks the boundaries of a day, you determine month's beginning and end.

At night you fascinate us earthlings as you move through your phases, reflecting the light of your superior soul mate.
He rules the day, you rule the night with your diffused light. Together you affect the ocean tides, causing spring tides and neap tides by your varied alignments.

You are believed by some to affect the mood of those we call lunatics.
While you move through your phases, they are calm, but when you are full, they turn raving mad.

Thou celestial cupid, who mesmerize lovers as they sit under the atmospheric canopy encircled by your silvery light.

Oh, ancient prophet, that signals the nearness of your Maker's return to earth.
You harbinger of tumultuous events. The ancients studied you to decipher your prognostications.

On this side of eternity, we revel in your beauty, because when time gives way to eternity, we will have no need of sun nor you for God your creator will be our source of light.

Author's note: This eulogy is an excerpt from the one I wrote for my mother's funeral. It is included in this book as a tribute to her and to give the readers a sneak peek into my life.

13. Eulogy for my Mother

Joyce Letitia Richmond-Solomon (A servant of God and a friend to man)
To everything there is a season and God has created each person for a special reason.
Blessed and happy are those who discover the reason for their existence,
Fulfilling their calling with passion and doing their duty with great diligence.
My mother Joyce Letitia Richmond-Solomon was indeed such a person.

A time to be born
Joyce aka Letitia was born on June 14, 1935 to the late Gershon Hanover and Sylverine Toney.
She was born prematurely, and her parents despaired for her life,
But she survived, thanks to God and to a devoted and caring midwife,
Her siblings were Escil, Humil, Mignon, Swetnam, Vernon, and Miriam.

A time to learn
Her formal education was received at the Ann's Grove Roman Catholic school.
Her childhood friend, Flora Dublin, recalls that Joyce was a brilliant and devoted student.
She passed the College of Preceptors examination and desired to become a certified teacher.
But her socioeconomic situation did not afford her this opportunity.

A time to love
Joyce was married to the late David Uriah Richmond and later to the late Alfred Solomon.
She invested her life in raising her nine children, eight of whom are still alive.

Her loving and caring extended beyond familial boundaries embracing strangers, neighbors, and friends.
Wherever she went people were attracted to her loving and winsome personality.

A time to live
Even though she did not work outside the home while her children were young, Joyce was very industrious. She raised fowls and other livestock and planted a garden to supplement the income of her husband. She was also a seamstress and was skillful with her hands, knitting various items to beautify her humble home and adorn her children.

She was also very active in serving the community through her church's outreach arm.
Her close friends admired her for being authentic, outspoken, humorous, kind, generous, and humble.
Music and poetry were an important part of her life, and morning and evening worship were part of the daily routine in her home. Her children were taught to memorize the scriptures and learn and sing the hymns of the Christian faith.

Joyce was a gifted writer. She wrote skits, poems and lyrics for songs and composed the music for the songs. I guess this is the source of my love of music and writing poetry and my winsome personality.

After suffering a stroke in March of 2009, she never fully recovered and was confined to her bed from that point until the time of her death. Though bedridden she was not sad or depressed. She stayed involved with her family and friends who would call on the phone or visit.
Birthday celebrations became an important feature in the later stages of her life. She loved to have her children, grandchildren, greatgrandchildren, other family members and friends around her on such occasions.

A time to die
On 26, 20017, the breath of life exited Joyce's body and returned to God who gave it, and her sojourn on earth ended at the age of eighty- two years, four months and twelve days.

She is survived by her siblings Escil, Mignon, sisters-in-law Patsy David, and Sheila Hanover, daughters-in law Roxanne Richmond, Leonette George-Richmond, and Collette Richmond, a large number of nieces, nephews, great nieces and nephews, cousins, brothers and sisters in Christ and friends.

Though dead, she lives vicariously through the lives of her eight children, (Ruth, Alvilda, David, Dawn, Donna, Claire, Ken, and William), her 35 grandchildren, 39 great grandchildren and two great greatgrandchildren.

Author's note: This poem was inspired by a series of radio programs on brokenness, that my wife and I listened on the radio. We were so impressed that we bought and read the book that was the basis for the radio broadcasts.

14. Brokenness

In the beginning it was not so. Adam and Eve were perfect when God's created them. Their interactions with each other reflected the perfection of the relationship between Father, Son and Holy Spirit.

They, like us were created with freedom of choice and could choose whether to follow God's plan for their lives or go their own way. When tempted by Satan, they chose to follow his suggestion and disobey God.

That act of disobedience fractured their relationship with God and with each other and resulted in the brokenness that we experience today.

Adam and Eve hid from God after their disobedience. This is the first evidence of Brokenness. We hide or try to hide our wrongdoing because we are Broken.

Confronted with his disobedience, Adam and Eve resorted to blame. He blamed God and, she blamed the serpent. Ever wondered why we are inclined to blame others for our mistakes. It is because we are Broken.

Many children are abandoned by one or sometimes both parents, who themselves were abandoned by one or both of their parents. The result of this is Brokenness in children who then grow into Broken adults.

Divorce, substance abuse, prostitution, sexual promiscuity, lesbianism, homosexuality, bisexuality, low self-esteem, pleasure-seeking, lying, cheating, stealing, killing, and a host of other dysfunctions are symptoms of humanity's Brokenness.

Where do we find help for our Brokenness? It begins with a choice. We know from experience that to keep our cars running well we need to follow the instructions in the Owner's Manual.

Follow the instructions and your car runs well and you get to enjoy it for a long time. Ignore the instructions and your car will finally break down and leave you stranded. The choice is yours.

After this Brokenness invaded God's plans for a perfect life for his creatures, he devised a plan to combat our Brokenness and finally accomplish humanity's healing and restoration.

Like cars, we have a Maker and he has provided us with an Owner's Manual, called the Bible. Read it and become familiar with God's plan for our healing and restoration.

By following his instructions, we can mitigate the effects of our Brokenness. When we ignore his instructions, we experience areas of break down in our life. The choice is ours. Brokenness or Healing and Restoration.

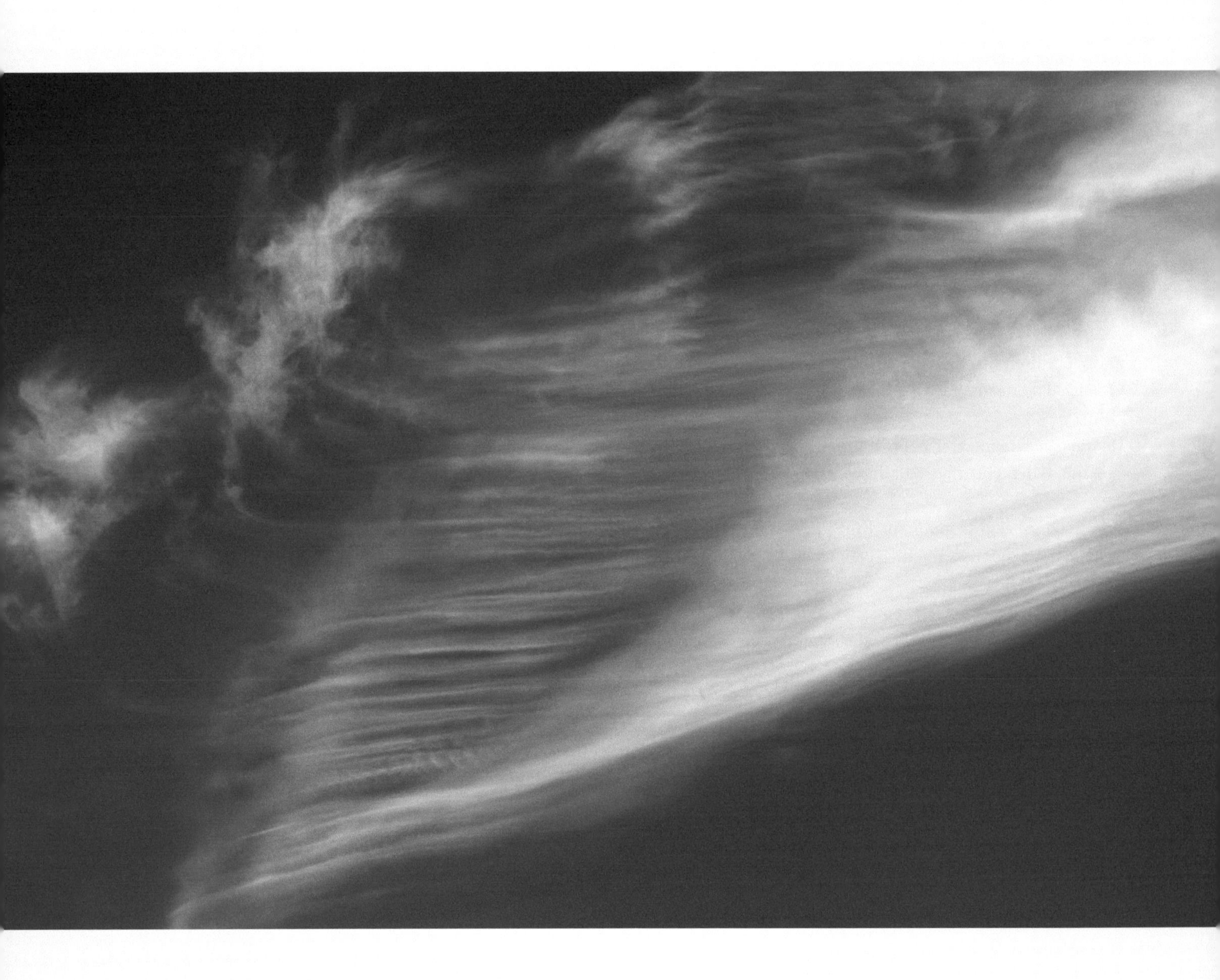

Author's note: I was inspired to write the poem as I reflected on the death of my mother and several other individuals in close succession. As I thought about death, I was reminded of the Bible passage 1 Cor. 15:54 which lifted my spirit and gave me hope.

15. Death's Demise

Clothed in deception you made your entrance at the dawn of earth's history.
Sin gave you access to the world and humanity cannot fathom your mystery.
You are the product of disobedience, but the deceiver promised Eve enlightenment.
When Cain killed Abel, you claimed your first victim much to your heart's content.

You have a penchant for claiming your victims en masse, as in the cataclysmic flood.
Whether men or women, young or old, you do not care, all you want is humanity's blood.
Your tools of trade are wars, famines, pestilences and genocide.
O how many victims you claim with suicide, infanticide, and other forms of homicide.

Like a tyrant you rule as day follow night, subduing your victims with your power and might.
But the resurrection of Lazarus should give you a hint that your end is surely in sight.
Your dominion is not complete, Moses and Elijah point to a future time of sweet relief.
That is soon to be realized by those who in Jesus place their firm belief.

In the fullness of time you met your match, when you came face to face with Jesus, God's Son.
You and the grave conspired to hold him fast, and if you succeeded the battle would be won.
Battered, bruised, and nailed to a cross, he said, "It is finished" and gave up the Ghost.
Then with Satan, demons, soldiers and sealed tomb you hoped to be his eternal host.

The day of your triumph was the Preparation Day called Friday
Then came the Sabbath, so in the tomb He decided to stay.
The first day we call Sunday dawned, and the prison tomb was still sealed.
But this was to be the day when Jesus' resurrection power was revealed.

He came forth from the tomb with life original and unborrowed.
Then mocked you because, by his victory you were swallowed,
His victory over you, **Death**, gives His children a life of assurance.
That one day they will praise Him, for their glorious deliverance.

Author's note: Living in the beautiful Pocono Mountains of Pennsylvania affords me the pleasure of enjoying nature. This poem was influenced by my experiences in this natural environment. I hope that as you read it you would develop a new appreciation for nature and gain a fresh perspective of the natural environment which surround you.

16. Nature's Symphony

As dark gives way to light and day begins to dawn the symphony of sounds begin.
First a single chirp from a lone bird, then a response from a mate in reply.
Then as if on cue, the other birds in the arena join in the antiphonal motif of call and reply.
And before long the entire orchestra of feathered creatures are engaged in a full-throated
chorus of praise to their Creator for the dawning of another day.

Next it is the sun's turn to serenade its Creator with sounds of praise quite different from the birds.
Within its bowels acoustic waves bounce from one side to another causing its surface to jiggle,
Much like the surface of a bell oscillates when struck by its tongue.
Though we cannot hear it, the sun is playing a secret melody as part of the natural universal symphony.

If we could hear the sound it would make our souls quake and eardrums brake because the frequency is so low that it throbs with a super-deep perpetual bass.
The sun not only sings, but it provides the lighting effects that serves as the backdrop for symphonic sounds that surround us all through the day.

Then there is the forest full of upright stick figures that look like caricatures of humans.
In winter they look like ghostly skeletons, in spring like young maidens in delicate dresses
that turn into full-flowing green robes in summer and colorful kimonos in fall.
They need the wind to make them sing. As the wind blows through their stems and leaves
it produces music so soothing and sweet.

At times, the notes are loud and shrill, like the sound of violins wafting up a hill.
But as the velocity of the wind decreases, the notes are more mellow and soothing.
Then to add contrast the wind blows much slower producing baritone and bass with such skill.
The occasional sound of a chirp, a bark, a howl, punctuates the score of this inspiring symphony.

Sometimes the conductor pulls out all the stops, and nature explodes with loud sounds that pop.
The winds howl and branches snap as trees sway, then the rain joins in the refrain, turning leaves
into tambourines and shakers.
An occasional thunderclap and lightning flash create a wild symphony that most surely rocks.

As creatures of the Creator's hand, we too must add our songs sublime,
By living for his glory now, we join with birds, sun, wind and trees,
And stars and mighty oceans wild, to daily raise our voices loud,
In thanks to God, for life and Son, as part of nature's symphony of praise.

Author's note: This poem was inspired by a series of sermons I heard on the radio by Dr. David Jeremiah. After listening to one of the sermons I decided to write this poem to address this issue which is so prevalent in modern society.

17. Loneliness

Experts describe it as a complex emotional reaction, felt by people dwelling in isolation.
Sufferers sometimes cannot explain what they are feeling, as loneliness possess their being.
Why, oh why, is this disease so pervasive among so vast a population?
What is the explanation for this strange phenomenon we are seeing?

The family structure is cracked and broken, and we seem to be losing our mind,
Emailing, texting and tweeting have replaced good, old-fashioned conversating.
Instead of loving, caring, bosom friends, we've settled for the Facebook kind.
And spend the best part of our day posting, streaming and Facetiming.

We've forsaken our Creator and dislodged our spiritual mooring.
Now devoid of all bearing, we spend our life drifting,
Searching for true meaning by carousing, feasting and lusting,
And end up frustrated, depressed and still wanting.

Singles are often lonely, and companionship is a deep need.
It is not fun to cook, eat, and sleep all by your lonely self.
But singles can beat loneliness if to this creed they give heed,
That, "No man is an island, entire of itself."

Wives can be lonely too, when companionship is lacking,
Because the man they married does not do much talking.
His home is his castle, and he behaves like he is a king,
The TV is his mistress and he does not do a thing.

Then there is the survivor, whose spouse is dead and gone,
And they are left to run the race and face life all alone.
The children have a life of their own, and time is scarce as gold,
So, time with them is but a dream after they leave the fold.

Now if we want to cure this strange phenomenon,
We must seek after God with humility and submission.
And find true satisfaction by modeling our mothers,
In loving and serving and caring for others.

Author's note: As a believer in Christ, I share his concern for the souls of men and women and for their total welfare. This poem is intended to help readers avoid the spiritual pitfall of rejecting God. If this poem causes you to think about matters pertaining to eternity and to accept God's provision of salvation, I would have accomplished my purpose.

18. Mock On or Repent

When the serpent said to Eve, "You shall not surely die,"
He knew to his breast that he was telling her a lie,
But this was the way Satan chose, God's image to mar,
As revenge for being cast out of heaven for causing war.

He wanted to mock God by undermining his authority,
And injecting his rebellious trait in all of humanity.
The history of the world bears witness to the fact,
That he was quite successful in employing this tact.

When God asked Cain and Abel sacrifices to make,
He was clear that only an animal sacrifice he would take,
Cain in defiance chose to offer fruits instead,
An evidence that the mocking trait was in his head.

God refused his offering, and Cain became depressed and sad,
And when Abel's offering was accepted, he really got mad.
But instead of repenting he let the anger boil in his head,
And when it was all over his brother Abel was dead.

As man became very sinful, God gave Noah a message of warning,
But instead of repenting, the Antediluvians started mocking,
Until the heavens opened and the deep fountains started flowing,
And except for Noah and his family, they all died by drowning.

In the fullness of time God sent His Son with a message of love,
He was anointed for His mission by the descent of a dove,
But instead of repenting the religious leaders resorted to mocking,
And when their mocking peaked, God's Son they were crucifying.

And what of us living today, at a time when the end is nearing,
When we hear of wars, famines, earthquakes, and flooding,
Do we find their frequency and prevalence to be alarming?
Or do we just shrug our shoulders and resort to mocking.

Citizens of the world caught up in the Coronavirus pandemic,
The evidence that our world is nearing an end is seismic,
Would you heed God's warning message and start repenting,
Or would you choose instead to keep on mocking?

Whatever your choice the consequences are clear,
God's message of warning is loud enough for all to hear,
Follow Satan and his mocking and reap a fiery destiny
Or choose Christ as your Savior and enjoy life for eternity.

Author's note: This poem was written on Mother's Day 2020 as a tribute to my deceased mother and to all mothers. I hope that the thoughts and sentiments expressed are shared by readers all over the world and that they will share this poem with their mothers for many years into the future.

19. A Tribute to the True Heroes - MOTHERS

In the beginning when God decided a new race to create,
He gave Adam and Eve the ability to procreate.
With God as Creator and Adam as father,
Eve was destined the nations of the world to mother.

The serpent so subtle and cunning caused Eve to sin,
And in that very moment the dying process did begin,
As punishment God said Adam's life would be toilful,
And the process of childbirth for Eve would be painful.

Eve was so elated when she gave birth to her firstborn son Cain,
But little did she know that he would be the cause of much pain.
Soon after she birthed her second son named Abel,
He obeyed God's command, but against God Cain did rebel.

When God refused his offering, he let anger boil up in his head,
And when it was all over his brother Abel was dead,
Even as his birth brought joy to his mother Eve,
His violence against his brother caused her heart to grieve

Though our mothers the perfection of Eve do not possess,
We their children throughout our lives must confess,
They surely inherited all her maternal qualities,
As evidenced by our mothers' numerous abilities.

They carry us for nine months often in great discomfort,
And then endure the physical torture of childbirth.
After we are born a lifetime of nurture and caring commences,
Often in the face of many obstacles and sundry offences.

The roles mothers perform are too many to number,
Nurse, wife, chef, chauffeur, broken heart mender,
Psychologist, teacher, referee, entertainer, nutritionist,
Homemaker, judge, law enforcer and home economist.

When God established the family and roles for its members designed,
An important and special role to mothers he wisely assigned.
This multifaceted role requiring such skill, could be filled by no other,
Than, the indefatigable, amazing, and loving person we call mother.

So, on this day that has been devoted to the honoring of mothers,
We pay tribute to mothers who are devoted to caring for others,
And whether they are healthy or sick or alive or dead,
We will never let the memory of them fade from our head.

Author's note: At the time I was inspired to write this poem, I was engaged in a systematic study of a periodical on the Bible. I was so impressed by what I was learning that I wanted to share some of the content with others who may not have access to this material. It is my sincere hope that readers will take a second look at this ancient book and discover its relevance and transforming power for themselves.

20. The Bible

Compiled by human writers over a period of more than one millennium,
The Bible was written by men under the influence of a divine medium,
Having as its theme, Jesus - the author of the plan of salvation,
Its message is relevant to men and women of every tribe and nation.

Skeptics and scoffers have tried to dismiss it as a work of fiction,
And scholars and rulers have conspired to bring about its extinction,
Yet the Bible, though ancient, remains as relevant as ever,
With an influence on humanity that no power on earth can sever.

From Genesis to Revelation its messages all agree,
This is because it was inspired by the Mysterious Three,
Within its pages no contradiction is to be found,
For its content by a common theme is bound.

Where else can such amazing prophecies be found,
Which grasp the attention and leave readers spellbound.
Making believers of skeptics all the world around,
With their power to inspire faith and to confound.

For years many questioned its accuracy when speaking of history,
But the validity of its content is now being revealed by archaeology,
Time and again the truth of the Bible has been proven,
By scientists whom to doubt were previously given.

At one time the scholars believed and taught that the earth was flat,
And as far as they were concerned, this was just a matter of fact,
They laughed when the Bible spoke of the earth as being round,
But later its teachings were found to be both accurate and sound.

The Bible has had a profound and pervasive effect on human culture,
Influencing science, art, music, legal systems, language, and sculpture,
Wherever in the world you look, you cannot escape the power of this Book,
But desiring to get rid of the Bible, our sages have its teachings forsook.

My counsel to all the citizens of this world, is to open your mind and take a good look,
And if you are honest, you will have to conclude, that the Bible is indeed a unique book.
For in its pages God's plan of salvation for humanity is found,
Which helps us escape the wrath to come and live with him in eternity safe and sound.

Author's note: As a believer in Christ, I share his concern for the souls of men and women and for their total welfare. This poem was written to capture the essence of God's plan to rescue humanity from sin and provide a way for us to escape ultimate destruction. If it causes you to think about matters pertaining to eternity and to accept God's provision of salvation, I would have accomplished my purpose.

21. God's Plan of Salvation

When earth was engulfed in the amniotic fluid of mother abyss,
Your power moved upon the surface of the primeval depths,
Like the coordinated contractions of myocytes in the uterine walls,
And the earth emerged like a baby expelled from its mother's womb.

After the race You created was plunged into a spiritual abyss by sin,
It was time for You to demonstrate Your creative power once again.
Man's act of rebellion did not surprise you because you had a plan,
Before earth's foundation redemption was conceived for fallen man.

In the fullness of time You sent Your Son, implanted in a virgin's womb,
Like Adam's race He must experience the darkness of the watery tomb,
And then be expelled by the powerful contractions of the uterine wall,
Because the purpose of His coming was to rescue man from the fall.

From the moment He was born, the battle with evil was enjoined,
Many infants were killed by Herod while attempting to destroy Him,
O what cruel irony that one needing rescue would seek to kill his rescuer,
And that the redeemer will be annihilated by those He came to save.

From the height of the cross, He was then placed in a dark tomb,
Reminiscent of His condescension from heaven to sinful earth,
But death could not restrain the Creator of heaven and earth and life,
On first day of the week, He arose, triumphant over death.

So, for us lost and wretched creatures, trapped in a prison of sin.
There is good news in the offing for the Savior is about to return,
Not as babe in a manger, but as Lord of Lords and King of Kings,
With healing and salvation in His glorious and mighty wings.

To accept God's plan of salvation and experience peace and joy within,
You must turn from your life of rebellion, and accept His sacrifice for your sin,
And then the Holy Spirit He will give you, to guide, transform and help you,
To gain victory over sin and be ready to spend eternity with Him.

Author's note: I love the story of creation as recorded in the first book in the Bible, aptly named Genesis, because it records the story of the beginning of the world. This poem was written to capture the essence of the story in poetic form and stimulate readers to read the full narrative in the Bible.

22. *Creation According to Genesis*

Among the theories of origins, the Genesis account stands as chief,
Logical, coherent, and concise, among its peers it stands in stark relief,
Its poetic style, elegant literary structure, and distinctive motif,
Contribute to an account that for millions today still inspire belief.

The astronauts of Apollo 8, on the eve of the celebration of Christ's birth,
Read the words, "In the beginning God created the heavens and the earth"
These words are the foundation for the account of creation that will follow,
And as you read the narrative you will discover it does not sound hollow.

On day one of creation, God almighty commanded light to appear and it did,
And as he beheld the light he had just created, my God was so delighted,
Then by his might he separated the darkness from the light,
Naming the light part Day and the part with the darkness Night.

On day two of creation, the record states that God created the firmament,
And as a good parent would sometimes do to prevent any future argument,
He separated the waters that were above from waters that were below,
And at the end of day two of creation everything was perfect and mellow.

God was not done with the waters that were below the firmament,
He felt that they needed some further arrangement.
On day three, he gathered them together the Seas to birth,
And caused dry land to appear which he named Earth.

The earth looked naked and in God's mind it needed a little decoration,
So, on day three He created all the flowers and beautiful vegetation.
He spoke and from the earth came grasses and herbs of all description,
And fruit trees of every kind, to satisfy our hunger and cause salivation.

The Creator knew that the dark firmament would be a very dismal sight,
Therefore, on day four the stars were made the firmament to give light.
A lesser light, the moon, was created to dominate the sky at night,
And a greater light, the sun, by day to rule the heaven with its might.

Being a God of variety, on day five of creation he added some new features,
At his command, the waters teemed with a vast array of living creatures.
He designated the vast space between earth and sky,
As a domain where birds and other winged creatures can fly.

On day six it was the time for the Creator's crowning act.
He carefully scooped up some earth, and with great tact,
Created the man Adam in his own image. Then with a rib from his side,
Made the woman Eve, desiring they will forever in His presence abide.

Creation was completed and it was time for God to cease creating and rest,
So, he declared everything good, and the seventh day sanctified and blest.
And since the number seven is a symbol of His quintessence,
He decided to fill the seventh day with His divine holy presence.

His Name shall be called

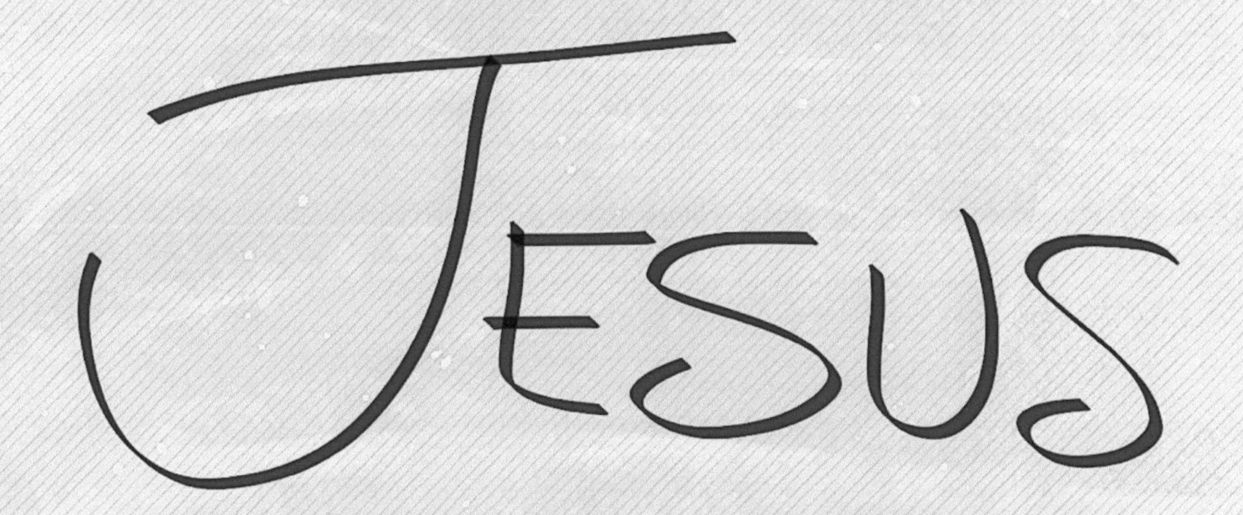

for he shall save His people from their sins.

Author's note: As a Christian I am fascinated by Jesus and His example of ultimate self-sacrifice informs my decisions and daily inspires my life. This poem is an attempt to capture the essence of His amazing life in poetic form. As with the poem on creation, it is my hope that this poem will stimulate readers to read the full account of the life of Jesus as recorded in the books Matthew, Mark, Luke and John in the Bible.

23. Jesus

When the beloved disciple named John wrote in the first line of his gospel book,
He was writing to his Jewish people because over time their God they forsook,
"In the beginning was the Word, and the Word was with God, and the Word was God,"
Was a reference to Jesus coming, sent by the Father, in fulfillment of his word.

From John's book we learn that you were the one speaking the word at the world's creation,
And that as a part of the divine plan, you had come to bring fallen mankind salvation.,
So, you laid aside your divinity and became one with humanity,
To thereby provide a way for sinful man to live with God in eternity.

By a miraculous process you were implanted in the womb of virgin meek and mild,
And at the end of a period of nine months, you were born as Mary's infant child.
That the one without beginning could be born and held in his mother's bosom,
Is a mystery too great for our finite and degenerate human minds to fathom.

As a human child you increased in wisdom and stature and gained favor with God and man,
There was no doubt in your mind that your purpose on earth was to fulfill your Father's plan,
Which involved you dying for our sins, after perfectly obeying all that His holy laws demand.
O what condescension on your part, to accomplish the salvation of fallen humankind.

Among those born of women there will never be one like you on earth,
Its history is subdivided into B.C., the period before your birth,
And A.D., the period after, erroneously interpreted by many as "after death."
Your powerful influence extends across this world's entire breadth.

Jesus, centuries after you have come and gone, your name is still a cause of offense,
There are those who reject you as a fraud, and those who come to your defense,
One group surrender their will and accept you as the God of their salvation,
While the other steadfastly refuse to submit to your loving dominion.

Before ascending to heaven, you promised one day to return,
To receive those who through the Holy Spirit have been reborn,
So, in faith we await the salvation that was from eternity planned,
And one day go home with you to dwell in that heavenly land.

Author's note: This poem was inspired by the murder of George Floyd by a police officer in Minneapolis, Minnesota on May 25,2020 and the scenes of protests, looting and vandalism that dominated television screens for weeks after.

24. The Deep Roots of Racism

When God created this world, everything was nice and dandy and perfect,
But the disobedience of Adam and Eve introduced sin and sowed defect,
Soon thereafter sin manifested itself as envy, hatred, and murder,
As their first son named Cain, killed Abel his younger brother.

With the passage of time human beings became wicked beyond belief,
Causing God their creator great sorrow and giving him much grief,
So great was the wickedness of his creatures made of flesh and blood,
That he made the decision to destroy them with a worldwide flood.

And when the Tower of Babel became the symbol of mankind's rebellion,
God changed his common language, and this resulted in much confusion,
Then he scattered the descendants of Noah across the face of earth,
And so, from Shem, Ham and Japheth, the nations of men were birth.

Wars periodically erupted as mankind became more and more corrupted,
The stronger nations soon dominated, and the weaker were subjugated,
Society became very stratified, and men and women were classified,
And the wealthy and educated were deemed chosen and magnified.

Laws and systems were put in place to perpetuate the stratified state,
Resulting in sporadic rebellion and producing a festering hate.
Sometimes there were moments when it seemed the old order will topple,
And be replaced by one that favored the majority of the people.

But even after these great movements, humans continued to segregate,
And before long society returned to the stratified state,
With a new order that in many ways the old one did imitate,
Resulting in new rebellion by people trying to change their fate.

In modern times a new and dreadful form of human segregation was introduced,
And people with dark skin, made in God's image, were by a system reduced,
To a race exploited, despised, humiliated, rejected, abused, subjugated,
And stripped of the dignity with which by the creator they were invested.

They were sold by some of their own sinful and greedy rulers,
Or captured by white, armed, cold-hearted human traffickers,
Then crammed into the cargo hold of a captain's merchant vessel,
And those who survived the harrowing journey, were sold as chattel.

After hundreds of years of this despicable trafficking in human lives,
Which destroyed stable families by separating husbands and wives,
Through the efforts of abolitionists both white and black,
The evil of institutionalized slavery was abolished by a legislative act.

But the laws and the systems remain which perpetuate the stratified state,
And this is compounded by the problem of sin and of festering hate,
Which as human beings we either tolerate or find difficult to eradicate,
So, everyone must join the struggle with the black race to change their fate.

While the deaths of hundreds of blacks in police custody makes us all annoyed,
People in America and the world over are outraged by the killing of George Floyd,
The usual voices of protest and condemnation are chanting and ranting,
But soon the news cycle would continue with its mind-numbing politicking.

If we ever hope the condition and fate of blacks in America to change,
We must all unite as Americans, and inspired by our outrage,
Begin a process of honest dialogue, that uncovers the truth, and bring reconciliation,
Then we must gradually dismantle the system that perpetuates racial discrimination.

Photo taken by author in Luray Caverns

Author's note: This poem was inspired by what the Bible teaches on this important and sometimes controversial subject. I challenge the readers to conduct their research so they can learn the truth about the Sabbath. Scientists have discovered what is called the circaseptan rhythm in our bodies which reveals that on every seventh day the week our bodies need rest so it can repair and restore itself.

25. The Sabbath

According to Genesis, after the six days of creation, God the Creator did rest,
And the seventh day he declared to be sanctified and holy and blest.
Adam was given the noble work of taking care of God's creation,
But because God had already worked, his first day was spent in relaxation.

After delivering his people from Egyptian slavery, God led them into the wilderness.
He protected and fed them for forty years and came to their aid in times of distress.
Each day he supplied them with manna, and on day six a double supply was provided,
Because on day seven of each week, no manna was on the ground to be collected.

At Mt Sinai when the ten commandments God did set forth,
The seventh day sabbath was included as the fourth,
Mankind was commanded to work six days with diligence and zest,
But on the seventh day, by God's order he was to take a rest.

When Jesus came and lived on earth, our salvation to arrange,
He rested on the seventh day, the law of God he did not change.
The four Gospels show that he obeyed the precepts of the decalogue,
By worshipping on the seventh day with others in the synagogue.

And after his work on earth was done, and Jesus went back to heaven,
His followers continued to work six days and to rest on day seven.
If Jesus had changed the Sabbath commandment as many claim,
His early disciples and followers would have been privy to the same.

For centuries after Christ, they kept the Sabbath even when persecuted,
So, when was the change of the seventh day Sabbath instituted?
At first Sunday was designated as a day of rest, much like a holiday,
But finally, the papacy decreed that it should replace God's sabbath day.

Many ask how we can be sure that Saturday is the seventh day,
So, let us take a careful look at what the Bible in Luke has to say,
The day when Jesus was crucified was called the day of preparation,
And the first day of the week, was the day of his resurrection.

We call the day of his crucifixion Good Friday,
And the day of his resurrection Easter Sunday,
The day in between we call Saturday,
And the Bible in Luke calls it the Sabbath day.

There are efforts today to change the order of the calendar days,
And make Monday the first day of the week, to suit man's ways,
Making Sunday the seventh day, the Sabbath of his invention,
But man's machination, cannot change the Sabbath of God's creation.

One day soon we will all have a major decision to make,
Whether to obey God, or the mark of the beast to take.
So, today Jesus pleads with you to give him your allegiance,
Because if you do not, to the Beast you will give obeisance.

Printed in the United States
By Bookmasters